MICHIGAN RULES OF EVIDENCE
2024 Edition

Updated through February 1, 2024

Michigan Legal Publishing Ltd.
QUICK DESK REFERENCE SERIES™

Table of Contents

Article I

Rule 101 Scope; Definitions

(a) **Scope**. These rules govern proceedings in Michigan courts. The specific courts and proceedings to which the rules apply, along with exceptions, are set out in Rule 1101.

(b) **Statutory Rules**. A statutory rule of evidence not in conflict with these rules or other rules adopted by the Supreme Court is effective until superseded by a Supreme Court rule or decision.

(c) **Definitions**. In these rules:

    (1) "civil case" means a civil action or proceeding;

    (2) "criminal case" includes a criminal proceeding;

    (3) "public office" includes a public agency;

    (4) "record" includes a memorandum, report, or data compilation;

    (5) a "rule prescribed by the Supreme Court" means a rule adopted by the Michigan Supreme Court; and

    (6) a reference to any kind of written material or any other medium includes electronically-stored information.

Rule 102 Purpose

These rules should be construed so as to administer every proceeding fairly, eliminate unjustifiable expense and delay, and promote the development of evidence law, to the end of ascertaining the truth and securing a just determination.

Rule 103 Rulings on Evidence

(a) **Preserving a Claim of Error**. A party may claim error in a ruling to admit or exclude evidence only if the error affects a substantial right of the party and:

    (1) if the ruling admits evidence, a party, on the record:

        (A) timely objects or moves to strike; and

        (B) states the specific ground, unless it was apparent from the context; or

    (2) if the ruling excludes evidence, a party informs the court of its substance by an offer of proof, unless the substance was apparent from the context.

(b) **Not Needing to Renew an Objection or Offer of Proof**. Once the court rules definitively on the record—either before or at trial—a party need not renew an objection or offer of proof to preserve a claim of error for appeal.

(c) **Court's Statement About the Ruling; Directing an Offer of Proof**. The court may make any statement about the character or form of the evidence, the objection made, and the ruling. The court may direct that an offer of proof be made in question-and-answer form.

(d) **Preventing the Jury from Hearing Inadmissible Evidence**. To the extent practicable, the court must conduct a jury trial so that inadmissible evidence is not suggested to the jury by any means.

(e) **Taking Notice of Plain Error**. A court may take notice of a plain error affecting a substantial right, even if the claim of error was not properly preserved.

Rule 104 Preliminary Questions

(a) **In General**. The court must decide any preliminary question about whether a witness is qualified, a privilege exists, or evidence is admissible. In so deciding, the court is not bound by evidence rules, except those on privilege.

(b) **Relevance That Depends on a Fact**. When the relevance of evidence depends on whether a fact exists, proof must be introduced sufficient to support a finding that the fact does exist. The court may admit the proposed evidence on the condition that the proof be introduced later.

(c) **Conducting a Hearing so That the Jury Cannot Hear it**. The court must conduct any hearing on a preliminary question so that the jury cannot hear it if:

    (1) the hearing involves the admissibility of a confession;

    (2) a defendant in a criminal case is a witness and so requests; or

(3) justice so requires.

(d) **Cross-Examining a Defendant in a Criminal Case**. By testifying on a preliminary question, a defendant in a criminal case does not become subject to cross-examination on other issues in the case.

(e) **Evidence Relevant to Weight and Credibility**. This rule does not limit a party's right to introduce before the jury evidence that is relevant to the weight or credibility of other evidence.

Rule 105 Limiting Evidence That is Not Admissible Against Other Parties or for Other Purposes

If the court admits evidence that is admissible against a party or for a purpose—but not against another party or for another purpose—the court, on timely request, must restrict the evidence to its proper scope and instruct the jury accordingly.

Rule 106 Remainder of or Related Writings or Recorded Statements

If a party introduces all or part of a writing or recorded statement, an adverse party may require the introduction, at that time, of any other part—or any other writing or recorded statement—that in fairness ought to be considered at the same time.

Article II

Rule 201 Judicial Notice of Adjudicative Facts

(a) **Scope**. This rule governs judicial notice of an adjudicative fact only, not a legislative fact.

(b) **Kinds of Facts That May Be Judicially Noticed**. The court may judicially notice a fact that is not subject to reasonable dispute because it:

    (1) is generally known within the trial court's territorial jurisdiction; or

    (2) can be accurately and readily determined from sources whose accuracy cannot reasonably be questioned.

(c) **Taking Notice**. The court may take judicial notice on its own and may require a party to supply the necessary information.

(d) **Timing**. The court may take judicial notice at any stage of the proceeding.

(e) **Opportunity to Be Heard**. On timely request, a party is entitled to be heard on the propriety of taking judicial notice and the nature of the fact to be noticed. If the court takes judicial notice before notifying a party, the party, on request, is still entitled to be heard.

(f) **Instructing the Jury**. In a civil case, the court must instruct the jury to accept the noticed fact as conclusive. In a criminal case, the court must instruct the jury that it may or may not accept the noticed fact as conclusive.

Rule 202 Judicial Notice of Law

(a) **When Discretionary**. A court may take judicial notice on its own of the following:

    (1) the common law, constitutions, and public statutes in force in every state, territory, and jurisdiction of the United States;

    (2) private acts and resolutions of the United States Congress and the Michigan Legislature;

(3) ordinances and regulations of Michigan governmental subdivisions or agencies; and

(4) the laws of foreign countries.

(b) **When Conditionally Mandatory**. A court must take judicial notice of each matter in subrule(a) if a party so requests and:

(1) supplies the court with sufficient information to enable it to properly comply with the request; and

(2) gives each adverse party such notice as the court may require to enable the adverse party to meet the request.

Article III

Rule 301 Presumptions in Civil Cases

In a civil case, unless a statute or these rules provide otherwise, the party against whom a presumption is directed has the burden of producing evidence to rebut the presumption. But this rule does not shift the burden of persuasion, which remains on the party who had it originally.

Rule 302 Presumptions in Criminal Cases

(a) **Scope**. In a criminal case, this rule governs a presumption against a defendant that is recognized at common law or is created by statute, including statutory provisions that certain facts are prima facie evidence of other facts or of guilt.

(b) **Instructing the Jury**. When a presumed fact against a defendant is submitted to the jury, the court must instruct the jury that:

    (1) it may or may not conclude from the basic facts that the presumed fact is true; and

    (2) the prosecution still bears the burden of proof beyond a reasonable doubt of all the elements of the offense.

Article IV

Rule 401 Test for Relevant Evidence

Evidence is relevant if:

(a) it has any tendency to make a fact more or less probable than it would be without the evidence; and

(b) the fact is of consequence in determining the action.

Rule 402 General Admissibility of Relevant Evidence

Relevant evidence is admissible unless any of the following provides otherwise:

- the United States Constitution;
- the Michigan Constitution;
- these rules; or
- other rules prescribed by the Supreme Court. Irrelevant evidence is not admissible.

Rule 403 Excluding Relevant Evidence for Prejudice, Confusion, Waste of Time, or Other Reasons

The court may exclude relevant evidence if its probative value is substantially outweighed by a danger of one or more of the following: unfair prejudice, confusing the issues, misleading the jury, undue delay, wasting time, or needlessly presenting cumulative evidence.

Rule 404 Character Evidence; Other Crimes, Wrongs, or Acts

(a) **Character Evidence**.

   (1) *Prohibited Uses*. Evidence of a person's character or character trait is not admissible to prove that on a particular occasion the person acted in accordance with the character or trait.

   (2) *Exceptions for a Defendant or Victim in a Criminal Case*. The following exceptions apply in a criminal case:

(A) a defendant may offer evidence of the defendant's pertinent trait, and if the evidence is admitted, the prosecutor may offer evidence to rebut it;

(B) in a homicide case, when self-defense is an issue, the defendant may offer evidence of the alleged victim's trait for aggression, and if the evidence is admitted, the prosecution may:

    (1) offer evidence of the defendant's same trait, and

    (2) offer evidence of the alleged victim's trait for peacefulness to rebut evidence that the alleged victim was the first aggressor; and

(C) in a criminal-sexual-conduct case, the defendant may offer evidence of:

    (1) the alleged victim's past sexual conduct with the defendant, and

    (2) specific instances of sexual activity showing the source or origin of semen, pregnancy, or disease.

(3) *Exceptions for a Witness.* Evidence of a witness's character may be admitted under Rules 607, 608, and 609.

(b) **Other Crimes, Wrongs, or Acts**.

(1) *Prohibited Uses.* Evidence of any other crime, wrong, or act is not admissible to prove a person's character in order to show that on a particular occasion the person acted in accordance with the character.

(2) *Permitted Uses.* If it is material, the evidence may be admissible for another purpose, such as proving motive, opportunity, intent, preparation, scheme, plan, or system in doing an act, knowledge, identity, absence of mistake, or lack of accident.

(3) *Notice in a Criminal Case.* In a criminal case, the prosecutor must:

(A) provide notice of any such evidence that the prosecutor intends to offer at trial, so that the defendant has a fair opportunity to meet it;

   (B) articulate in the notice the permitted purpose for which the prosecutor intends to offer the evidence and the reasoning that supports the purpose; and

   (C) do so in writing at least 14 days before trial, unless the court, for good cause, excuses pretrial notice, in which case the notice may be submitted in any form.

(4) *Requiring Defendant's Theory of the Case.* If necessary to determine the admissibility of evidence under this rule, the court must require the defendant to state the theory or theories of defense, limited only by the defendant's privilege against self-incrimination.

Rule 405 Methods of Proving Character

(a) **By Reputation or Opinion**. When evidence of a person's character or character trait is admissible, it may be proved by testimony about the person's reputation or by testimony in the form of an opinion. On cross-examination of the character witness, the court may allow an inquiry into relevant specific instances of the person's conduct.

(b) **By Specific Instances of Conduct**. When a person's character or character trait is an essential element of a charge, claim, or defense, the character or trait may also be proved by relevant specific instances of the person's conduct.

Rule 406 Habit; Routine Practice

Evidence of a person's habit or an organization's routine practice may be admitted to prove that on a particular occasion the person or organization acted in accordance with the habit or routine practice. The court may admit this evidence regardless of whether it is corroborated or whether there was an eyewitness.

Rule 407 Subsequent Remedial Measures

When measures are taken that would have made an event less likely to occur, evidence of subsequent measures is not admissible to prove negligence or culpable conduct in connection with the event.

But the court may admit this evidence for another purpose, such as impeachment or—if disputed—proving ownership, control, or the feasibility of precautionary measures.

Rule 408 Compromise Offers and Negotiations

(a) **Prohibited Uses**. Evidence of the following is not admissible to either prove or disprove the liability for or the validity or amount of a disputed claim:

    (1) furnishing, promising, or offering—or accepting, promising to accept, or offering to accept—a valuable consideration in compromising or attempting to compromise the claim; and

    (2) conduct or a statement made during compromise negotiations.

(b) **Exceptions**. If this evidence is otherwise discoverable, it need not be excluded merely because it is presented during compromise negotiations. And it need not be excluded if admitted for another purpose, such as proving a witness's bias or prejudice, negating a contention of undue delay, or proving an effort to obstruct a criminal investigation or prosecution.

Rule 409 Offers to Pay Medical and Similar Expenses

Evidence of furnishing, promising to pay, or offering to pay medical, hospital, or similar expenses resulting from an injury is not admissible to prove liability for the injury.

Rule 410 Pleas, Plea Discussions, and Related Statements

(a) **Prohibited Uses**. In a civil or criminal case, evidence of the following is not admissible against the defendant who made the plea or participated in the plea discussions:

    (1) a guilty plea that was later withdrawn or vacated;

    (2) a nolo contendere plea—except that, to the extent that evidence of a guilty plea would be admissible, evidence of a nolo contendere plea to a criminal charge may be admitted in a civil proceeding to defend against a claim asserted by the person who entered the plea;

(3) a statement made during a proceeding on either of those pleas under MCR 6.302 or MCR 6.310, a comparable state procedure, or Fed R Crim P 11; or

(4) a statement made during plea discussions with an attorney for the prosecuting authority if the discussions did not result in a guilty plea or they resulted in a later-withdrawn or vacated guilty plea.

(b) **Exceptions**. The court may admit a statement described in subrule (a)(3) or (4):

(1) in any proceeding in which another statement made during the same plea or plea discussions has been introduced, if in fairness the statements ought to be considered together; or

(2) in a criminal proceeding for perjury or false statement, if the defendant made the statement under oath, on the record, and with counsel present.

Rule 411 Liability Insurance

Evidence that a person was or was not insured against liability is not admissible to prove whether the person acted negligently or otherwise wrongfully. But the court may admit this evidence for another purpose, such as proving a witness's bias or prejudice or—if controverted—proving agency, ownership, or control.

Article V

Rule 501 Privilege in General

The common law governs a claim of privilege, unless a statute or court rule provides otherwise.

Article VI

Rule 601 Competency to Testify in General

Every person is competent to be a witness unless:
(a) the court finds, after questioning, that the person does not have sufficient physical or mental capacity or sense of obligation to testify truthfully or understandably; or
(b) these rules provide otherwise.

Rule 602 Need for Personal Knowledge

A witness may testify to a matter only if evidence is introduced sufficient to support a finding that the witness has personal knowledge of the matter. Evidence to prove personal knowledge may consist of the witness's own testimony. This rule does not apply to a witness's expert testimony under Rule 703.

Rule 603 Oath or Affirmation to Testify Truthfully

Before testifying, a witness must give an oath or affirmation to testify truthfully. It must be in a form designed to impress that duty on the witness's conscience.

Rule 604 Interpreter

An interpreter must be qualified and must give an oath or affirmation to make a true translation.

Rule 605 Judge's Competency as a Witness

The presiding judge may not testify as a witness at the trial. A party need not object to preserve the issue.

Rule 606 Juror's Competency as a Witness

(a) **At the Trial**. A juror may not testify as a witness before the other jurors at the trial. A party need not object to preserve the issue.

(b) **During an Inquiry into the Validity of a Verdict or Indictment**.

    (1) *Prohibited Testimony or Other Evidence*. During an inquiry into the validity of a verdict or indictment, a juror may not testify about any statement made or incident that occurred during the jury's deliberations; the effect of anything on that juror's or another juror's vote; or any juror's mental processes concerning the verdict or indictment. The court may not receive a juror's affidavit or evidence of a juror's statement on these matters.

    (2) *Exceptions*. A juror may testify about whether:

        (A) extraneous prejudicial information was improperly brought to the jury's attention;

        (B) an outside influence was improperly brought to bear on any juror; or

        (C) a mistake was made in entering the verdict on the verdict form.

Rule 607 Who May Impeach a Witness

Any party, including the party that called a witness, may attack the witness's credibility.

Rule 608 A Witness's Character for Truthfulness or Untruthfulness

(a) **Reputation or Opinion Evidence**. A witness's credibility may be attacked or supported by testimony about the witness's reputation for having a character for truthfulness or untruthfulness, or by testimony in the form of an opinion about that character. But evidence of truthful character is admissible only after the witness's character for truthfulness has been attacked.

(b) **Specific Instances of Conduct**. Except for a criminal conviction under Rule 609, extrinsic evidence is not admissible to prove specific instances of a witness's conduct in order to attack or support the witness's character for truthfulness. But the court may, on cross-examination, allow them to be inquired into if they are probative of the character for truthfulness or untruthfulness of:

(1) the witness; or

(2) another witness whose character the witness being cross-examined has testified about.

By testifying on another matter, a witness does not waive any privilege against self- incrimination for testimony that relates only to the witness's character for truthfulness.

Rule 609 Impeachment by Evidence of a Criminal Conviction

(a) **In General**. This rule applies to attacking a witness's character for truthfulness by evidence of a criminal conviction. The evidence is admissible if it has, during cross- examination, been elicited from the witness or established by public record and the following conditions are also met:

(1) the crime contained an element of dishonesty or false statement; or

(2) the crime contained an element of theft; and

　(A) in the convicting jurisdiction, the crime was punishable by imprisonment for more than one year or by death; and

　(B) the court determines that the evidence has significant probative value on character for truthfulness and—if the witness is the defendant in a criminal trial—that the probative value outweighs any prejudicial effect.

(b) **Determining Probative Value and Prejudicial Effect**. In determining probative value, the court must consider only the age of the conviction and the degree to which it indicates character for truthfulness. If a determination of prejudicial effect is required, the court must consider only the conviction's similarity to the charged offense and the possible effects on the decisional process if admitting the evidence causes the defendant to elect not to testify. The court must articulate, on the record, the analysis of each factor.

(c) **Time Limit**. Evidence of a conviction under this rule is not admissible if more than ten years have passed since the date of the conviction or of the witness's release from the confinement for it, whichever is later.

(d) **Effect of a Pardon, Annulment, or Certificate of Rehabilitation**. Evidence of a conviction is not admissible if:

   (1) the conviction has been the subject of a pardon, annulment, certificate of rehabilitation, or other equivalent procedure based on a finding that the person has been rehabilitated, and the person has not been convicted of a later crime punishable by death or imprisonment for more than one year; or

   (2) the conviction has been the subject of a pardon, annulment, or other equivalent procedure based on a finding of innocence.

(e) **Juvenile Adjudications**. Evidence of a juvenile adjudication is admissible under this rule if it is offered in a later case against that same child in the family division of circuit court. Otherwise, the evidence is admissible only if:

   (1) it is offered in a criminal case or in a juvenile proceeding against the child;

   (2) the adjudication was of a witness other than the child;

   (3) an adult's conviction for that offense would be admissible to attack the adult's credibility; and

   (4) admitting the evidence is necessary to fairly determine the case or proceeding.

(f) **Pendency of an Appeal**. A conviction that satisfies this rule is admissible even if an appeal is pending. Evidence of the pendency is also admissible.

Rule 610 Religious Beliefs or Opinions

Evidence of a witness's religious beliefs or opinions is not admissible to attack or support the witness's credibility.

Rule 611 Mode and Order of Examining Witnesses and Presenting Evidence

(a) **Control by the Court; Purposes**. The court must exercise reasonable control over the mode and order of examining witnesses and presenting evidence so as to:

    (1) make those procedures effective for determining the truth;

    (2) avoid wasting time; and

    (3) protect witnesses from harassment or undue embarrassment.

(b) **Appearance of Parties and Witnesses**. The court must exercise reasonable control over the appearance of parties and witnesses so as to:

    (1) ensure that the fact-finder can see and assess their demeanor; and

    (2) ensure their accurate identification.

(c) **Scope of Cross-Examination**. A witness may be cross-examined on any matter relevant to any issue in the case, including credibility. But the judge may limit cross-examination regarding matters not testified to on direct examination.

(d) **Leading Questions**.

    (1) *When Allowed*. Leading questions should not be used on direct examination except as necessary to develop a witness's testimony. Ordinarily, the court should allow leading questions:

        (A) on cross-examination; and

        (B) when a party calls a hostile witness, an adverse party, or a witness identified with an adverse party.

    (2) *Intent to Ask Not Required*. It is not necessary to declare the intent to ask leading questions before the questioning begins or before the questioning moves beyond preliminary inquiries.

Rule 612 Writing or Object Used to Refresh a Witness

(a) **Scope**. This rule gives an adverse party certain options when a witness uses a writing or object to refresh memory:
   (1) while testifying; or
   (2) before testifying, if practicable and the court decides that justice requires the party to have those options at the trial, hearing, or deposition in which the witness is testifying.

(b) **Adverse Party's Options; Deleting Unrelated Matter**. An adverse party is entitled to have the writing or object produced, to inspect it, to cross-examine the witness about it, and to introduce in evidence—for its bearing on credibility only unless otherwise admissible under these rules—any portion that relates to the witness's testimony. If the producing party claims that the writing or object includes unrelated matter, the court must examine it in camera, remove any unrelated portion, and order that the rest be delivered to the adverse party. Any portion removed over objection must be preserved for the record.

(c) **Failure to Produce or Deliver the Writing or Object**. If a writing or object is not produced or is not delivered as ordered, the court may issue any appropriate order. But if the prosecution does not comply in a criminal case, the court must strike the witness's testimony or,—if justice so requires—declare a mistrial.

Rule 613 Witness's Prior Statement

(a) **Showing or Disclosing the Statement During Examination**. When examining a witness about the witness's prior statement, whether written or not, a party need not show it or disclose its contents to the witness. But the party must, on request, show it or disclose its contents to an adverse party's attorney or the witness.

(b) **Extrinsic Evidence of a Prior Inconsistent Statement**. Extrinsic evidence of a witness's prior inconsistent statement is admissible only if the witness is given an opportunity to explain or deny the statement and an adverse party is given an opportunity to examine the witness about it, or if justice so requires. This subrule does not apply to an opposing party's statement under Rule 801(d)(2).

Rule 614 Court's Calling or Examining a Witness

(a) **Calling**. The court may call a witness on its own or at a party's request. Each party is entitled to cross-examine the witness.
(b) **Examining**. The court may examine a witness regardless of who calls the witness.
(c) **Objections**. A party may object to the court's calling or examining a witness either at that time or at the next opportunity when the jury is not present.

Rule 615 Excluding Witnesses

At a party's request, the court may order witnesses excluded so that they cannot hear other witnesses' testimony. Or the court may do so on its own. But this rule does not authorize excluding:
(a) a party who is a natural person;
(b) an officer or employee of a party that is not a natural person, after being designated as the party's representative by its attorney; or
(c) a person whose presence a party shows to be essential to presenting the party's claim or defense.

Article VII

Rule 701 Opinion Testimony by Lay Witnesses

If a witness is not testifying as an expert, testimony in the form of an opinion is limited to one that is:
(a) rationally based on the witness's perception; and
(b) helpful to clearly understanding the witness's testimony or to determining a fact in issue.

Rule 702 Testimony by Expert Witnesses

A witness who is qualified as an expert by knowledge, skill, experience, training, or education may testify in the form of an opinion or otherwise if:
(a) the expert's scientific, technical, or other specialized knowledge will help the trier of fact to understand the evidence or to determine a fact in issue;
(b) the testimony is based on sufficient facts or data;
(c) the testimony is the product of reliable principles and methods; and
(d) the expert has reliably applied the principles and methods to the facts of the case.

Rule 703 Bases of an Expert

An expert may base an opinion on facts or data in the case that the expert has been made aware of or personally observed. The facts or data must be in evidence—or, in the court's discretion, be admitted in evidence later.

Rule 704 Opinion on an Ultimate Issue

An opinion is not objectionable just because it embraces an ultimate issue.

Rule 705 Disclosing the Facts or Data Underlying an Expert's Opinion

Unless the court orders otherwise, an expert may state an opinion—and give the reasons for it—without first testifying to the underlying facts or data. But the expert may be required to disclose those facts or data on cross-examination.

Rule 706 Court-Appointed Expert Witnesses

(a) **Appointment Process**. On a party's motion or on its own, the court may order the parties to show cause why expert witnesses should not be appointed and may ask the parties to submit nominations. The court may appoint any expert that the parties agree on and any of its own choosing. But the court may only appoint someone who consents to act.

(b) **Expert's Role.** The court must inform the expert of the expert's duties. The court may do so in writing and have a copy filed with the clerk or may do so orally at a conference in which the parties have an opportunity to participate. The expert:
  (1) must advise the parties of any findings the expert makes;
  (2) may be deposed by any party;
  (3) may be called to testify by the court or any party; and
  (4) may be cross-examined by any party, including the party that called the expert.

(c) **Compensation**. The expert is entitled to a reasonable compensation, as set by the court. The compensation is payable as follows:
  (1) in a criminal case or in a civil case involving just compensation under the Fifth Amendment, from any funds that are provided by law; and
  (2) in any other civil case, by the parties in the proportion and at the time that the court directs—and the compensation is then charged like other costs.

(d) **Disclosing the Appointment to the Jury**. The court may authorize disclosure to the jury that the court appointed the expert.

(e) **Parties' Choice of Their Own Experts**. This rule does not limit a party in calling its own experts.

Rule 707 Use of Learned Treatises for Impeachment

To the extent called to an expert witness's attention on cross-examination, a statement is admissible for impeachment purposes only if:

- the statement is contained in a published treatise, periodical, or pamphlet;
- the publication is on a subject of history, medicine, or other science or art; and
- the publication is established as a reliable authority by the testimony or admission of the witness, by other expert testimony, or by judicial notice.

If admitted, the statement may be read into evidence but must not be received as an exhibit.

Article VIII

Rule 801 Definitions That Apply to Rules 801–807; Exclusions from Hearsay

The following definitions apply under Rules 801–807:

(a) **Statement**. "Statement" means a person's oral assertion, written assertion, or nonverbal conduct if the person intended it as an assertion.

(b) **Declarant**. "Declarant" means the person who made the statement.

(c) **Hearsay**. "Hearsay" means a statement that:

    (1) the declarant does not make while testifying at the current trial or hearing; and

    (2) a party offers in evidence to prove the truth of the matter asserted in the statement.

(d) **Statements That Are Not Hearsay**. A statement that meets the following conditions is not hearsay:

    (1) A *Declarant-Witness's Prior Statement*. The declarant testifies and is subject to cross-examination about a prior statement, and the statement:

        (A) is inconsistent with the declarant's testimony and was given under penalty of perjury at a trial, hearing, or other proceeding or in a deposition;

        (B) is consistent with the declarant's testimony and is offered to rebut an express or implied charge that the declarant recently fabricated it or acted from a recent improper influence or motive in so testifying; or

        (C) identifies a person as someone the declarant perceived earlier.

    (2) *An Opposing Party's Statement*. The statement is offered against an opposing party and:

        (A) was made by the party in an individual or representative capacity, except a statement made in connection with:

            (i) a guilty plea to a misdemeanor motor-vehicle violation; or

        (ii) an admission of responsibility for a civil infraction under a motor-vehicle law;

(B) is one the party manifested that it adopted or believed to be true

(C) was made by a person whom the party authorized to make a statement on the subject;

(D) was made by the party's agent or employee on a matter within the scope of that relationship and while it existed; or

(E) was made by the party's coconspirator during and in furtherance of the conspiracy, if there is independent proof of the conspiracy.

Rule 802 The Rule Against Hearsay

Hearsay is not admissible unless these rules provide otherwise.

Rule 803 Exceptions to the Rule Against Hearsay

The following are not excluded by the rule against hearsay, regardless of whether the declarant is available as a witness:

(1) **Present Sense Impression**. A statement describing or explaining an event or condition made while or immediately after the declarant perceived it.

(2) **Excited Utterance**. A statement relating to a startling event or condition, made while the declarant was under the stress of excitement that it caused.

(3) **Then-Existing Mental, Emotional, or Physical Condition**. A statement of the declarant's then-existing state of mind or emotional, sensory, or physical condition (such as intent, plan, motive, design, mental feeling, pain, or bodily health), but not including a statement of memory or belief to prove the fact remembered or believed unless it relates to the validity or terms of declarant's will.

(4) **Statement Made for Purposes of Medical Treatment or Diagnosis in Connection with Treatment**. A statement that:

      (A) is made for—and is reasonably necessary to—medical treatment or diagnosis in connection treatment; and

      (B) describes medical history, past or present symptoms or sensations, their inception, or their general cause.

(5) **Recorded Recollection**. A record that:

      (A) is on a matter the witness once knew about but now cannot recall well enough to testify fully and accurately;

      (B) was made or adopted by the witness when the matter was fresh in the witness's memory; and

      (C) accurately reflects the witness's knowledge.

      (D) If admitted, the record may be read into evidence but may be received as an exhibit only if offered by an adverse party.

(6) **Record of a Regularly Conducted Activity**. A record of an act, transaction, occurrence, event, condition, opinion, or diagnosis if:

      (A) the record was made at or near the time by—or from information transmitted by—someone with knowledge;

      (B) the record was kept in the course of a regularly conducted activity of a business, organization, occupation, or calling, whether or not for profit;

      (C) making the record was a regular practice of that activity;

      (D) all these conditions are shown by the testimony of the custodian or another qualified witness, or by a certification that complies with a rule prescribed by the Supreme Court or with a statute permitting certification; and

      (E) the opponent does not show that the source of information or the method or circumstances of preparation indicate a lack of trustworthiness.

(7) **Absence of a Record of a Regularly Conducted Activity**. Evidence that a matter is not included in a record described in subrule (6) if:

(A) the evidence is admitted to prove that the matter did not occur or exist;

(B) a record was regularly kept for a matter of that kind; and

(C) the opponent does not show that the possible source of the information or other circumstances indicate a lack of trustworthiness.

(8) **Public Record**. A record or statement of a public office if it sets out:

(A) the office's activities; or

(B) a matter observed while under a legal duty to report, but not including;

    (i) in a criminal case, a matter observed by law-enforcement personnel; and

    (ii) information to which the limitations in MCL 257.624 apply.

(9) **Public Record of Vital Statistics**. A record of a birth, death, or marriage, if reported to a public office in accordance with a legal duty.

(10) **Absence of a Public Record**. Testimony—or a certification under Rule 902 that diligent search failed to disclose a public record or statement if the testimony or certification is admitted to prove that:

(A) the record or statement does not exist; or

(B) a matter did not occur or exist, if a public office regularly kept a record or statement for a matter of that kind.

(11) **Record of Religious Organizations Concerning Personal or Family History**. A statement of birth, legitimacy, ancestry, marriage, divorce, death, relationship by blood or marriage, or other similar facts of personal or family history, contained in a regularly kept record of a religious organization.

(12) **Certificate of Marriage, Baptism, and Similar Ceremonies**. A statements of fact contained in a certificate:

(A) made by a person who is authorized by a religious organization or by law to perform the act certified;

(B) attesting that the person performed a marriage or similar ceremony or administered a sacrament; and

(C) purporting to have been issued at the time of the act or within a reasonable time after it.

(13) **Family Record**. A statement of fact about personal or family history contained in a family record, such as a Bible, genealogy, chart, engraving on ring, inscription on a portrait, or engraving on an urn, or burial marker.

(14) **Record of Document That Affects an Interest in Property**. The record of a document that purports to establish or affect an interest in property if:

(A) the record is admitted to prove the content of the original recorded document, along with its signing and its delivery by each person who purports to have signed it;

(B) the record is a record of a public office; and

(C) a statute authorizes recording documents of that kind in that office.

(15) **Statement in Document That Affects an Interest in Property**. A statement contained in a document that purports to establish or affect an interest in property if the matter stated was relevant to the document's purpose—unless later dealings with the property are inconsistent with the truth of the statement or the purport of the document.

(16) **Statement in Ancient Document**. A statement in a document that is at least 20 years old and whose authenticity is established.

(17) **Market Reports and Similar Commercial Publications**. Market quotations, lists, directories, or other compilations that are generally relied on by the public or by persons in particular occupations.

(18) **Deposition Testimony of an Expert**. A witness's testimony given in a lawful deposition during the same

proceeding if the court finds that the deponent is an expert witness and if the deponent is not a party to the proceeding.

(19) **Reputation Concerning Personal or Family History**. A reputation among a person's family by blood, adoption, or marriage—or among a person's associates or in the community—concerning the person's birth, adoption, legitimacy, ancestry, marriage, divorce, death, relationship by blood, adoption, or marriage, or similar facts of personal or family history.

(20) **Reputation Concerning Boundaries or General History**. A reputation in a community—arising before the controversy—concerning boundaries of land in the community or customs that affect the land, or concerning general historical events important to that community, state, or nation.

(21) **Reputation Concerning Character**. A reputation among a person's associates or in the community concerning the person's character.

(22) **Judgment of a Previous Conviction**. Evidence of a final judgment of conviction if:

   (A) the judgment was entered after a trial or guilty plea, but not a nolo contendere plea unless allowed by MRE 410;

   (B) the conviction was for a crime punishable by death or by imprisonment for more than a year;

   (C) the evidence is admitted to prove any fact essential to the judgment; and

   (D) when offered by the prosecutor in a criminal case for a purpose other than impeachment, the judgment was against the defendant.

   (E) The pendency of an appeal may be shown but does not affect admissibility.

(23) **Judgment Involving Personal, Family, or General History, or a Boundary**. A judgment that is admitted to prove a matter of personal, family, or general history, or boundaries, if the matter:

    (A) was essential to the judgment; and

    (B) could be proved by evidence of reputation.

Rule 803A Hearsay Exception; Child's Statement About a Sexual Act

(a) **Scope**. This rule applies in criminal and delinquency proceedings only.

(b) **Conditions**. A statement describing an incident that included a sexual act performed with or on the declarant by the defendant or an accomplice is admissible to the extent that it corroborates testimony given by the declarant during the same proceeding if:

    (1) the declarant was under the age of ten when the statement was made;

    (2) the statement is shown to have been spontaneous and without indication of manufacture;

    (3) either the declarant made the statement immediately after the incident or any delay is excusable as having been caused by fear or other equally effective circumstance;

    (4) the statement is introduced through the testimony of someone other than the declarant; and

    (5) the proponent of the statement makes known to the adverse party the intent to offer it and its particulars sufficiently before the trial or hearing to provide the adverse party with a fair opportunity to prepare to meet it.

If the declarant made more than one corroborative statement about the incident, only the first is admissible under this rule.

Rule 804 Exceptions to the Rule Against Hearsay–When the Declarant is Unavailable as a Witness

(a) **Criteria for Being Unavailable**. A declarant is considered to be unavailable as a witness if the declarant:

    (1) is exempted from testifying about the subject matter of the declarant's statement because the court rules that a privilege applies;

(2)   refuses to testify about the subject matter despite a court order to do so;

(3)   testifies to not remembering the subject matter;

(4)   cannot be present or testify at the trial or hearing because of death or a then- existing infirmity, physical illness, or mental illness; or

(5)   is absent from the trial or hearing, and

    (A) the statement's proponent has not been able, by process or other reasonable means, to procure:

        (i) the declarant's attendance, in the case of a hearsay exception under subrule (b)(1) or (6); or

        (ii) the declarant's attendance or testimony, in the case of a hearsay exception under subrule (b)(2), (3), or (4); and

    (B) in a criminal case, the proponent shows due diligence.

(6)   But this subrule (a) does not apply if the statement's proponent procured or wrongfully caused the declarant's unavailability as a witness in order to prevent the declarant from attending or testifying.

(b) **The Exceptions**. The following are not excluded by the rule against hearsay if the declarant is unavailable as a witness:

(1)   *Former testimony*. Testimony that:

    (A) was given as a witness at a trial or hearing whether given during the current proceeding or a different one; and

    (B) is now offered against a party who had—or, in a civil case, whose predecessor in interest had—an opportunity and similar motive to develop it by direct, or cross, or redirect examination.

(2)   *Deposition Testimony*. A witness's testimony given in a lawful deposition during the same or another proceeding, if the party against whom the testimony is now offered had—or in a civil case, a predecessor in interest had— an opportunity and similar motive to develop the testimony by direct, or cross, or redirect examination. For this

paragraph (2) only, "unavailability of a witness" also includes situations in which:

(A) the witness is more than 100 miles from the place of trial or hearing, or is out of the United States, unless it appears that the witness's absence was procured by the party offering the deposition; or

(B) on motion and notice, exceptional circumstances make it desirable— in the interests of justice and with due regard to the importance of presenting witnesses' testimony orally in open court—to allow the deposition to be used.

(3) *Statement Under the Belief of Imminent Death*. In a prosecution for homicide or in a civil case, a statement that the declarant, while believing the declarant's death to be imminent, made about its cause or circumstances.

(4) *Statement Against Interest*. A statement that:

(A) a reasonable person in the declarant's position would have made only if the person believed it to be true because, when made, it was so contrary to the declarant's proprietary or pecuniary interest or had so great a tendency to invalidate the declarant's claim against someone else or to expose the declarant to civil or criminal liability; and

(B) if the statement tends to expose the declarant to criminal liability and is offered to exculpate the accused, it must be supported by corroborating circumstances that clearly indicate its trustworthiness.

(5) *Statement of Personal or Family History*. A statement about:

(A) the declarant's own birth, adoption, legitimacy, ancestry, marriage, divorce, relationship by blood, adoption, or marriage, or similar facts of personal or family history, even though the declarant had no way of acquiring personal knowledge about that fact; or

    (B) another person concerning any of these facts, as well as death, if the declarant was related to the person by blood, adoption, or marriage or was so intimately associated with the person's family that the declarant's information is likely to be accurate.

  (6) *Statement Offered Against a Party That Wrongfully Caused or Encouraged the Declarant's Unavailability.* A statement offered against a party that wrongfully caused— or encouraged the declarant's unavailability as a witness, and did so intending that result.

Rule 805 Hearsay Within Hearsay

Hearsay within hearsay is not excluded by the rule against hearsay if each part of the combined statements conforms with an exception to the rule.

Rule 806 Attacking and Supporting the Declarant

When a hearsay statement—or a statement described in Rule 801(d)(2)(C), (D), or (E)—has been admitted in evidence, the declarant's credibility may be attacked, and then supported, by any evidence that would be admissible for those purposes if declarant had testified as a witness. The court may admit evidence of the declarant's inconsistent statement or conduct, regardless of when it occurred or whether the declarant had an opportunity to explain or deny it. If the party against whom the statement was admitted calls the declarant as a witness, the party may examine the declarant on the statement as if on cross-examination.

Rule 807 Residual Exception

(a) **In General**. Under the following conditions, a hearsay statement is not excluded by the rule against hearsay even if the statement is not admissible under a hearsay exception in Rule 803 or 804:

  (1) the statement has equivalent circumstantial guarantees of trustworthiness;

(2)   it is offered as evidence of a material fact;

(3)   it is more probative on the point for which it is offered than any other evidence that the proponent can obtain through reasonable efforts; and

(4)   admitting it will serve the purposes of these rules and the interests of justice.

(b) **Notice**. The statement is admissible only if the proponent gives an adverse party reasonable notice of the intent to offer the statement—including its substance and the declarant's name and address—so that the party has a fair opportunity to meet it.

Article IX

Rule 901 Authenticating or Identifying Evidence

(a) **In General**. To satisfy the requirement of authenticating or identifying an item of evidence, the proponent must produce evidence sufficient to support a finding that the item is what its proponent claims it is.

(b) **Examples**. The following are examples only—not a complete list—of evidence that satisfies the requirement:

    (1) *Testimony of Witness with Knowledge*. Testimony that an item is what it is claimed to be.

    (2) *Nonexpert Opinion About Handwriting*. A nonexpert's opinion that handwriting is genuine, based on a familiarity with it that was not acquired for the current litigation.

    (3) *Comparison by an Expert Witness or the Trier of Fact*. A comparison with an authenticated specimen by an expert witness or the trier of fact.

    (4) *Distinctive Characteristics and the Like*. The appearance, contents, substance, internal patterns, or other distinctive characteristics of an item, taken together with all the circumstances.

    (5) *Opinion About a Voice*. An opinion identifying a person's voice—whether heard firsthand or through mechanical or electronic transmission or recording—based on hearing the voice at any time under circumstances that connect it with the alleged speaker.

    (6) *Evidence About a Telephone Conversation*. For a telephone conversation, evidence that a call was made to the number assigned at the time to:

        (A) a particular person, if circumstances, including self-identification, show that the person was the one called; or

        (B) a particular business, if the call was made to a business and the call related to business reasonably transacted over the telephone.

    (7) *Evidence About Public Records*. Evidence that:

(A) a document was recorded or filed in a public office as authorized by law; or

(B) a purported public record or statement is from the office where items of this kind are kept.

(8) *Evidence About Ancient Documents or Data Compilation.* For a document or data compilation, evidence that it:

(A) is in a condition that creates no suspicion about its authenticity;

(B) was in a place where, if authentic, it would likely be; and

(C) is at least 20 years old when offered.

(9) *Evidence About a Process or System.* Evidence describing a process or system and showing that it produces an accurate result.

(10) *Methods Provided by a Statute or Rule.* Any method of authentication or identification allowed by a Michigan statute or a rule prescribed by the Supreme Court.

Rule 902 Evidence That Is Self-Authenticating

The following items of evidence are self-authenticating; they require no extrinsic evidence of authenticity in order to be admitted:

(1) **Domestic Public Document That is Sealed and Signed**. A document that bears:

(A) a seal purporting to be that of the United States; any state, district, commonwealth, territory, or insular possession of the United States; the former Panama Canal Zone; the Trust Territory of the Pacific Islands; a political subdivision of any of these entities; or a department, agency, or officer of any entity named above; and

(B) a signature purporting to be an execution or attestation.

(2) **Domestic Public Document That is Not Sealed but is Signed and Certified**. A document that bears no seal if:

(A) it bears the signature of an officer or employee of an entity named in subrule (1)(A); and

      (B) another public officer who has a seal and official duties within that same entity certifies under seal—or its equivalent—that the signer has the official capacity and that the signature is genuine.

(3) **Foreign Public Document**. A document that purports to be signed or attested by a person who is authorized by a foreign country's laws to do so. The document must be accompanied by a final certification that certifies the genuineness of the signature and official position of the signer or attester—or of any foreign official whose certificate of genuineness relates to the signature or attestation or is in a chain of certificates of genuineness relating to the signature or attestation. The certification may be made by a secretary of a United States embassy or legation; by a consul general, consul, vice consul, or consular agent of the United States; or by a diplomatic or consular official of the foreign country assigned or accredited to the United States. If all parties have been given a reasonable opportunity to investigate the document's authenticity and accuracy, the court may, for good cause, either:

      (A) order that it be treated as presumptively authentic without final certification; or

      (B) allow it to be evidenced by an attested summary with or without final certification.

(4) **Certified Copy of Public Record**. A copy of an official record—or a copy of a document that was recorded or filed in a public office as authorized by law—if the copy is certified as correct by:

      (A) the custodian or another person authorized to make the certification; or

      (B) a certificate that complies with subrules (1), (2), or (3) or a Michigan or federal statute.

(5) **Official Publication**. A book, pamphlet, or other publication purporting to be issued by a public authority.

(6) **Newspapers and Periodicals**. Printed material purporting to be a newspaper or periodical.

(7) **Trade Inscription and the Like**. An inscription, sign, tag, or label purporting to have been affixed in the course of business and indicating origin, ownership, or control.

(8) **Acknowledged Document**. A document accompanied by a certificate of acknowledgment that is lawfully executed by a notary public or another officer who is authorized to take acknowledgments.

(9) **Commercial Paper and Related Documents**. Commercial paper, a signature on it, and related documents, to the extent allowed by general commercial law.

(10) **Presumptions Under Law**. A signature, document, or anything else that a Michigan or federal statute declares to be presumptively or prima facie genuine or authentic.

(11) **Certified Domestic or Foreign Record of a Regularly Conducted Activity**. The original or a copy of a domestic or foreign record that meets the requirements of Rule 803(6)(A)-(C), as shown by a certification of the custodian or another qualified person that complies with a Michigan statute or a rule prescribed by the Supreme Court. Before the trial or hearing, the proponent must give an adverse party reasonable written notice of the intent to offer the record—and must make the record and certification available for inspection— so that the party has a fair opportunity to challenge them.

Rule 903 Subscribing Witness

A subscribing witness's testimony is necessary to authenticate a writing only if required by the law of the jurisdiction that governs its validity.

Article X

Rule 1001 Definitions That Apply to Rules 1001–1008

In Rules 1001–1008

(a) A "writing" consists of letters, words, numbers, or their equivalent set down in any form.

(b) A "recording" consists of letters, words, numbers, or their equivalent recorded in any manner.

(c) A "photograph" means a photographic image or its equivalent stored in any form.

(d) An "original" of a writing or recording means the writing or recording itself or any counterpart intended to have the same effect by the person who executed or issued it. For electronically-stored information, "original" means any printout—or other output readable by sight—if it accurately reflects the information. An "original" of a photograph includes the negative or any print from it.

(e) A "duplicate" means a counterpart produced by a mechanical, photographic, chemical, electronic, or other equivalent process or technique that accurately reproduces the original.

Rule 1002 Requirement of the Original

An original writing, recording, or photograph is required in order to prove its content unless these rules or a statute provides otherwise.

Rule 1003 Admissibility of Duplicates

A duplicate is admissible to the same extent as the original unless a genuine question is raised about the original's authenticity or the circumstances make it unfair to admit the duplicate.

Rule 1004 Admissibility of Other Evidence of Content

An original is not required and other evidence of the content of a writing, recording, or photograph is admissible if:

(a) all the originals are lost or destroyed, and not by the proponent acting in bad faith;

(b) an original cannot be obtained by any available judicial process;

(c) the party against whom the original would be offered had control of the original; was at that time put on notice, by pleadings or otherwise, that the original would be a subject of proof the trial or hearing; and fails to produce it at the trial or hearing; or

(c) the writing, recording, or photograph is not closely related to a controlling issue.

Rule 1005 Copies of Public Records to Prove Content

The proponent may use a copy to prove the content of an official record—or of a document that was recorded or filed in a public office as authorized by law—if these conditions are met: the record or document is otherwise admissible; and the copy is certified as correct in accordance with Rule 902(4) or is testified to be correct by a witness who has compared it with the original. If no such copy can be obtained by reasonable diligence, then the proponent may use other evidence to prove the content.

Rule 1006 Summaries to Prove Content

The proponent may use a summary, chart, or calculation to prove the content of voluminous writings, recordings, or photographs that cannot be conveniently examined in court. The proponent must make the originals or duplicates available for examination or copying, or both, by other parties at a reasonable time and place. And the court may order the proponent to produce them in court.

Rule 1007 Testimony or Statement of a Party to Prove Content

The proponent may prove the content of a writing, recording, or photograph by the testimony, deposition, or written statement of the party against whom the evidence is offered. The proponent need not account for the original.

Rule 1008 Functions of the Court and Jury

Ordinarily, the court determines whether the proponent has fulfilled the factual conditions for admitting other evidence of the content of a writing, recording, or photograph under Rule 1004 or 1005. But in a jury trial, the jury determines—in accordance with Rule 104(b)—any issue about whether:

(a) an asserted writing, recording, or photograph ever existed;

(b) another one produced at the trial or hearing is the original; or

(c) other evidence of content accurately reflects the content.

Article XI

Rule 1101 Applicability of the Rules

(a) **Rules Applicable**. Except as otherwise provided in subrule (b) or in a rule prescribed by the Supreme Court, these rules apply to all Michigan court actions and proceedings.

(b) **Rules Inapplicable**. The rules—except for those on privilege— do not apply to the following:

    (1) *Preliminary Questions of Fact*. The court's determination under Rule 104(a), on a preliminary question of fact governing admissibility.

    (2) *Grand Jury*. Proceedings before grand juries.

    (3) *Miscellaneous Criminal Proceedings*. Proceedings for extradition or rendition; sentencing; granting or revoking probation; issuing criminal summonses, arrest warrants, and search warrants; and proceedings for release on bail or otherwise.

    (4) *Contempt Proceedings*. Contempt proceedings in which the court may act summarily.

    (5) *Small Claims*. Proceedings in the small claims division of the district court.

    (6) *In Camera Custody Hearings*. In camera proceedings in child-custody matters to determine a child's custodial preference.

    (7) *Proceedings Involving Juveniles*. Proceedings in the family division of the circuit court whenever MCR subchapter 3.900 states that the Michigan Rules of Evidence do not apply.

    (8) *Preliminary Examinations–Property Matters*. At a preliminary examination in a criminal case, during which hearsay is admissible to prove the ownership, value, or possession of—or right to use or enter—property.

    (9) *Domestic Relations Matters*. The court's consideration of a report or recommendation submitted by the friend of the court under MCL 552.505(1)(g) or (h).

(10) *Mental-Health Hearings–Opinion Testimony*. In hearings under Chapters 4, 4A, 5, and 6 of the Mental Health Code, MCL 330.1400 et seq., during which the court may consider hearsay data that are part of the basis for the opinion presented by a testifying mental health expert.

Rule 1102 Title

These rules are named the Michigan Rules of Evidence and may be cited as MRE.